W9-BXT-935

4-18

BL 5.8 AR pts 1.0

Bremen Public Library
Bremen, Indiana

Stories of GREAT PEOPLE

Cleopatra's Coin

Gerry Bailey and Karen Foster

Illustrated by Leighton Noyes and Karen Radford

🌱 Crabtree Publishing Company

www.crabtreebooks.com

Mr. RUMMAGE has a stall piled high with interesting objects—and he has a great story to tell about each and every one of his treasures.

DIGBY PLATT is an antique collector. Every Saturday he picks up a bargain at Mr. Rummage's antique stall and loves listening to the story behind his new 'find'.

HANNAH PLATT is Digby's argumentative, older sister—and she doesn't believe a word that Mr. Rummage says!

CHRISSY's vintage clothing stall has all the costumes Digby and Hannah need to act out the characters in Mr. Rummage's stories.

Mr. CLUMPMUGGER has an amazing collection of ancient maps, dusty books, and old newspapers in his rare prints stall.

Crabtree Publishing Company

www.crabtreebooks.com

Other books in the series

Shakespeare's quill

Columbus's chart

Martin Luther King, Jr's microphone

Leonardo's palette

Armstrong's moon rock

The Wright Brothers' glider

Marco Polo's silk purse

Mother Teresa's alms bowl

Sitting Bull's tomahawk

Credits

Cover image: Charles Walker/Topham
AKG Images: 15 bottom right, 21 bottom right, 24 top left
British Museum, London/Werner Forman: 18 right
British Museum, London/HIP/Topham: 16 bottom left, 18 center left
British Museum, London/Eileen Tweedy/Art Archive: 28 bottom right
Charles Walker/Topham: 13 right, 32 top right
Dahesh Museum of Art, New York, USA/Bridgeman Art Library: 16 top right
Egyptian Museum, Cairo/Dagli Orti/Art Archive: 32 bottom right
Egyptian Museum, Cairo/Andrea Jemolo/AKG Images: 10 top right
Erich Lessing/AKG Images: 18 bottom left, 23 center right, 27 center right
Fitzwilliam Museum, Cambridge/Werner Forman: 10 center right
Fotomas/Topham: 15 top left
Mary Evans Picture Library: 15 top right, 24 center right, 28 bottom left, 29 bottom left, 31 bottom right
Musée du Louvre, Paris/Dagli Orti/Art Archive: 13 center left, 35 bottom right
Musée du Louvre, Paris/Erich Lessing/AKG Images: 17 bottom
Musée de la Revolution Francaise, Vizille, France/Bridgeman Art Library: 20 bottom right
Picturepoint/Topham: 9 top left
Roger-Viollet/Topham: 11 top left
R. Sheridan/Ancient Art & Architecture Collection: 29 top right
Vatican Museums/AKG Images: 27 bottom left
Villa Barbarigo, Noventa Vicentina, Italy/Giraudon/Bridgeman Art Library: 26 top right

Picture research: Diana Morris info@picture-research.co.uk

Library and Archives Canada Cataloguing in Publication

Bailey, Gerry
        Cleopatra's coin / Gerry Bailey and Karen Foster ; illustrated by Leighton Noyes and Karen Radford.

(Stories of great people)
Includes index.
ISBN 978-0-7787-3685-1 (bound).--ISBN 978-0-7787-3707-0 (pbk.)

        1. Cleopatra, Queen of Egypt, d. 30 B.C.--Juvenile fiction.
2. Queens--Egypt--Biography--Juvenile fiction. 3. Egypt--History--332-30 B.C.--Juvenile fiction. I. Foster, Karen, 1959- II. Noyes, Leighton III. Radford, Karen IV. Title. V. Series.

PZ7.B15Cl 2008   j823'.92   C2007-907614-9

Library of Congress Cataloging-in-Publication Data

Bailey, Gerry.
  Cleopatra's coin / Gerry Bailey and Karen Foster ; Illustrated by Leighton Noyes and Karen Radford.
        p. cm. -- (Stories of great people)
  Includes index.
  ISBN-13: 978-0-7787-3685-1 (rlb)
  ISBN-10: 0-7787-3685-7 (rlb)
  ISBN-13: 978-0-7787-3707-0 (pb)
  ISBN-10: 0-7787-3707-1 (pb)
  1. Cleopatra, Queen of Egypt, d. 30 B.C.--Juvenile literature. 2. Queens--Egypt--Biography--Juvenile literature. I. Foster, Karen, 1964- II. Noyes, Leighton. III. Radford, Karen IV. Title. V. Series.
  DT92.7.B23 2008
  932'.021092--dc22
  [B]
                                        2007051249

Crabtree Publishing Company

www.crabtreebooks.com   1-800-387-7650

Published in Canada
Crabtree Publishing
616 Welland Ave.
St. Catharines, Ontario
L2M 5V6

Published in the United States
Crabtree Publishing
PMB16A
350 Fifth Ave., Suite 3308
New York, NY 10118

Published by CRABTREE PUBLISHING COMPANY
Copyright © **2008** Diverta Ltd.

All rights reserved. No part of this publication may be reproduced, stored in a retrieval system or be transmitted in any form or by any means, electronic, mechanical, photocopying, recording, or otherwise, without the prior written permission of Crabtree Publishing Company.

Cleopatra's Coin

Table of Contents

Every Saturday morning, Knicknack Market comes to life. The street vendors are there almost before the sun is up. And by the time you and I are out of bed, the stalls are built, the boxes opened, and all the goods are carefully laid out on display.

Objects are piled high. Some are laid out on velvet: precious necklaces and jeweled swords. Others stand upright at the back:

large, framed pictures of very important people, lamps made from tasseled satin, and old-fashioned cash registers—the kind that jingle when the drawers are opened.

And then there are things that stay in their boxes all day, waiting for the right customer to come along: war medals laid out in straight lines, or utensils in polished

silver for all those special occasions.

But Mr. Rummage's stall is different. Mr. Rummage of Knicknack Market has a stall piled high with a disorderly jumble of things that no one could ever want.

Who wants to buy a stuffed mouse? Or a broken umbrella? Or a pair of false teeth?

Mr. Rummage has them all. And, as you can imagine, they don't cost a lot!

Rummage's Antiques

This is why Digby comes to Mr. Rummage's stall every Saturday morning. Digby Platt collects antiques. At the age of exactly ten and three quarters, Digby has a collection of antiques that would leave you breathless. He has more antiques than anyone of his age you're ever likely to meet. And, in case you hadn't guessed already, Digby Platt—Antique Collector Extraordinaire— is a very close friend of Mr. Rummage.

Mr. Rummage saves all his best bargains for Digby. At least that's what Digby believes, for why else would William Shakespeare's quill, Florence Nightingale's first aid box, or Marco Polo's map of Silk Road be sitting there unsold?

Today, while he sorts through the mounds of junk in search of a bargain, Digby's older sister Hannah watches with a scowl. She doesn't believe a word Mr. Rummage says!

"Well, I never!" said Mr. Rummage, as the boy held up an old coin.

"That's a real find. And I'd forgotten it was there, Digby."

"It's just an old penny," said Hannah, scornfully.

"Oh no," said Mr. Rummage slowly. "That's a very valuable coin. Do you know whose portrait that is stamped on the front? It's the head of a powerful queen who lived 2,000 years ago. Cleopatra VII of Egypt took on the power of the Roman Empire and became one of the most famous women in history."

Cleopatra

THERE ARE FEW RECORDS OF HOW CLEOPATRA LOOKED. ROMAN STATUES OF HER, AS WELL AS SOME COINS, MAKE HER APPEAR STRONG AND MANLY, WITH A HOOKED NOSE.

No one knows exactly what Cleopatra was like because much of her story was told by Roman historians, who wrote about her after her death. They described Cleopatra as a seductress and an all-around crafty woman. But the Romans had conquered Egypt and so they weren't very complimentary! What we do know is that she was intelligent, a skillful ruler, and devoted to her country. She was exceptionally clever even as a child, and managed to survive in a family where brothers and sisters were prepared to murder each other to gain power. Cleopatra was smart enough to influence both people and events in order to get what she wanted. But was she the scheming woman the Romans said she was?

The coin that Digby found

This coin was minted during the reign of Cleopatra VII and shows her face on one side. Only about ten coins in good condition still exist from Cleopatra's reign. Her silver coins didn't actually contain much silver. They were made mostly of bronze. That's because her weak, flute-playing father gave most of the country's cash to the Romans to keep their armies out of Egypt.

Let's find out...

EGYPTIAN CARVINGS SHOW HER WITH DELICATE FEATURES AND BEAUTIFUL EYES. BUT WHATEVER CLEOPATRA LOOKED LIKE, SHE WAS CERTAINLY A FASCINATING WOMAN WHO MADE A VERY POWERFUL IMPRESSION.

Royal family

Cleopatra belonged to the powerful Ptolemy family. The Ptolemies came to power after the death of Alexander the Great of Macedonia, who conquered Egypt in 323 B.C. Ptolemy the Great was a good ruler, but once he died, murder, **bribery**, and **corruption** became the order of the day. By the time Cleopatra came along, the Ptolemies weren't a happy family at all.

CLEOPATRA'S NAME

As a Ptolemy, she had a birth name and a throne name. Cleopatra was her **Macedonian** birth name. And her Egyptian throne name was Netjeret mer-it-es, which means "Goddess, Beloved of Her Father".

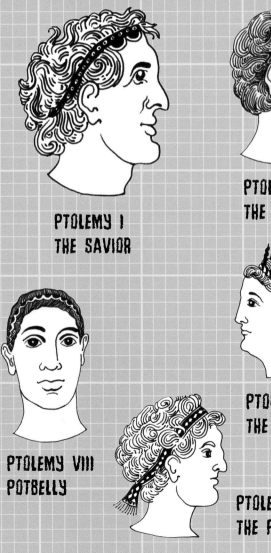

**PTOLEMY I
THE SAVIOR**

**PTOLEMY II
THE SCHOLAR**

**PTOLEMY VIII
POTBELLY**

**PTOLEMY III
THE BENEFACTOR**

**PTOLEMY XII
THE FLUTE PLAYER**

FIT FOR A QUEEN

When she was crowned, Cleopatra received the symbols of a pharaoh: a golden crook, a whip, and a **scepter**. She wore linen robes and ceremonial leather clothing. A special band of gold called a uraeus was placed on her head. On it was a cobra—the guardian snake of Egypt.

"Of course Cleopatra wasn't always a queen," continued Mr. Rummage. "She was once a little princess with a lot of brothers and sisters, just like your sister here."

"Huh!" said Hannah, who still didn't believe a word of it.

"But when Cleopatra was 18 years old, her father, Ptolemy XII, died. Cleopatra was crowned, and her younger brother, who was only 12, became king.

"She married her brother?" squealed Hannah, curling up her nose in disgust.

"Well, that was the way of the pharaohs," laughed Mr. Rummage. "But there was another reason for marrying your sister."

"I can't think of one," said Digby.

"Because they were pharaohs they were considered to be gods. And only a god could marry another god," Mr. Rummage went on. "So a sister had to marry a brother, or some other member of the family."

"I'm glad I'm not an Egyptian god," said Hannah smugly.

"Fat chance!" said Digby.

Mr. Rummage grinned.

"**B**efore Cleopatra came to power, she saw her sister killed and her father fall into debt to the wealthy Romans across the Mediterranean Sea. She knew she needed powerful friends among the Egyptian people if she was going to survive and keep her throne. But her family were Macedonian and they only spoke Greek. So Cleopatra learned Egyptian, the language of the people. She probably also learned eight other languages to prepare herself to take power."

"I'm glad I don't have to learn Egyptian," said Digby with a grimace.

"I'll say! You've got a long way to go before you will have learned your own language!" snorted Hannah.

"Now now, you two," Mr. Rummage winked. "Cleopatra was clever in other ways too. She made herself even more powerful in the people's eyes by calling herself the sun-god's daughter, and she also got the support of the priests. In fact, she had a beautiful temple built for her personal god, Isis, in the capital city of Alexandria."

"That's so cool!" exclaimed Hannah.

"I wouldn't mind having a personal god to make all my wishes come true."

"No kidding!" said Digby.

AMUN-RE, THE SUN GOD

The most powerful and important god was Amun-Re, the sun god. Amun-Re was the giver of life, the god of the air and fertility. The Amun part of his name means "the hidden one." Re was his supreme "sun god" name.

ANUBIS   **THOTH**   **HATHOR**

OTHER IMPORTANT GODS WERE ANUBIS, THE GOD OF MUMMIFICATION, WHO HAD A JACKAL'S HEAD; THOTH, WHO WAS REPRESENTED BY A BIRD CALLED AN IBIS; AND HATHOR, THE GODDESS OF MOTHERHOOD, WHO PROTECTED EGYPTIAN QUEENS.

Daughter of the sun

Cleopatra, like all pharaohs before her, was considered to be a goddess. Egyptians believed that many other gods came to Earth in the form of animals. When priests carried out sacred rituals, they often wore animal masks to depict a particular god or goddess. They wanted the common folk to believe they were the real thing!

ISIS, CLEOPATRA'S PROTECTOR-GODDESS

Isis became the most important goddess for most Egyptians. She was often shown with wings because the kite, a hook-beaked bird of prey, was sacred to her. Egyptians saw her as a good, kind goddess who loved all creatures. The pharaohs considered her their true mother. She was looked upon as both a wife and a mother goddess.

Egyptian temples were built as homes for the gods. Priests made offerings of food and flowers and burned sweet-smelling incense for sacred statues every day. Cleopatra gave lavish gifts to her temples to encourage the priests to support her.

"Was this city Alexandria where Cleopatra had her palace?" asked Hannah.

"It was indeed," said Mr. Rummage. "Alexandria was a splendid city on the shores of the Mediterranean Sea. It was founded by Alexander the Great and became the capital city of Egypt in 331 B.C."

"But why did he build it there?" asked Digby.

"Well, he thought the narrow strip of land sticking out into the sea would make a great harbor. You see, Egypt was trading with other countries. That's where its wealth came from, and its ships needed a large port to dock in. Alexander got an architect to draw up plans for the new city and..."

"Hi Mr. Clumpmugger," said Hannah, to the owner of the rare prints stall who was strolling by. "Are you interested in Cleopatra, too?"

"I am," answered Mr. Clumpmugger.

"But I'm even more interested in Alexandria. In fact, I've got a great map of the old city right here." And with that Mr. Clumpmugger spread out the map for his friends to read.

The PHAROS of PTOLOMY KING of EGYPT.

Alexandria

Alexandria, Cleopatra's home, was a bustling port on the Mediterranean Sea. The wide city streets were lined with exotic palms. The main street, called the Canopic, ran east to west and was almost 100 feet, (30 m) wide. North of it rose the royal palace and the Museion, which housed the artists and scholars of the day. Beyond lay the tombs of Alexander the Great and all the Ptolemies. To the south lay mighty temples, public buildings, and a vast athletics gymnasium. Alexandria was such a beautiful city, it was called "the shining pearl of the Mediterranean."

THE MAGNIFICENT PHAROS LIGHTHOUSE WAS THE FIRST THING VISITORS SAW AS THEY APPROACHED ALEXANDRIA. IT WAS BUILT BY PTOLEMY II IN THE 3RD CENTURY B.C. THE BUILDING WAS MORE THAN 323 FEET (100 M) HIGH AND SURROUNDED BY GARDENS. ON TOP WAS A STATUE OF THE GOD ZEUS THAT SPUN AROUND ABOVE A BURNING BEACON OF FIRE.

THE GREAT LIBRARY HOUSED OVER 100,000 PAPYRUS SCROLLS: A COPY OF ALMOST EVERY BOOK IN THE WORLD.

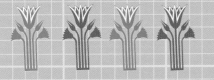

Splendid palace

Cleopatra's palace looked over the Great Harbor of Alexandria. She had a good view from her balcony. The dazzling white buildings with tall columns were surrounded by beautiful, scented gardens. In the heat of the day, Cleopatra would stroll along shaded walkways cooled by sea breezes. And later, she'd sit in her temple courtyards with their showy peacocks, elegant fountains, and pools filled with blue and white lotus flowers.

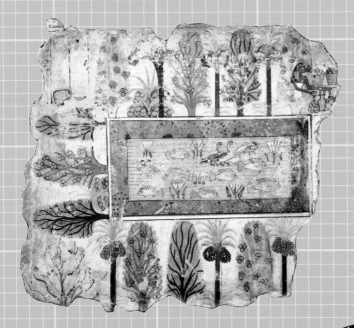

THE ROYAL ZOO

Cleopatra probably had her own zoo, with rare and exotic animals like lions, tigers, leopards, and bears. These would have been gifts from wealthy rulers of African and eastern kingdoms. The animals were kept as pets and paraded around the royal gardens on gold chains, decked in jewels and finery.

CLEOPATRA'S APARTMENTS

Cleopatra lived a life of luxury. Her royal apartments had floors of precious stones like **onyx** and **alabaster**, and the walls were hung with purple and gold tapestries. She could recline on silken couches or put her feet up on footstools of citrus wood. And when she needed anything, there were slaves standing by to obey her commands.

PALACE ENTERTAINERS

Dancers, acrobats, jesters, and minstrels entertained Cleopatra during the long, hot afternoons. Harps, **lutes**, and **lyres** were favorite instruments for banquets and parties.

Princess of the Nile

Without the great river Nile, the amazing civilizations of ancient Egypt could not have existed. For thousands of years, Eygptians lived in towns and villages beside its waters. Beyond its lush, green banks stretched hot, dry desert or the shores of the salty Mediterranean Sea.

EGYPT'S SUPER-HIGHWAY

The river Nile was a huge transportation system. Sailing along the river was much quicker and safer than traveling across the desert. It allowed Egyptian **merchants** to visit other lands where they could trade goods and bring back riches to please their pharaohs, including Cleopatra—who had very expensive tastes!

EACH SUMMER, RAINS CAME AND THE NILE BURST ITS BANKS. THICK, FERTILE MUD COVERED THE SURROUNDING FARMLAND, MAKING CROPS AND VINEYARDS GROW TALL AND STRONG.

FUN ON THE RIVER

The Nile was a source of entertainment. People relaxed by the river, went on riverboat outings, fished and swam. Cleopatra organized lavish hunting parties to catch crocodiles and hippopotamuses, as she traveled downriver on her royal boat.

"Cleopatra was so lucky," said Hannah as she waved goodbye to Mr. Clumpmugger. "All those palaces, gardens, pets, and parties..."

"Oh, it wasn't always easy," said Mr. Rummage. "Not everyone in Egypt was wealthy. People living along the Nile could be very poor. During Cleopatra's reign there were two years of **drought** and bad harvests that caused poverty and near starvation."

"But she was rich," said Hannah. "So why didn't she help out?"

"Cleopatra had a lot of problems, Hannah." answered Mr. Rummage. "She wanted power but so did her brother, and there were plenty of clashes and arguments."

"Just like us!" said Digby.

"And that's where your coin comes in, Digby. Cleopatra had coins minted that showed her head and not her brother's. That made him really angry. Trouble was, he was too young to rule and he let himself be guided by guardians. These schemers wanted all the power to themselves. They even tried to kidnap his strong-minded sister."

"Everyone wanted power," said Hannah.

"Exactly!" continued Mr. Rummage. "And things became so dangerous that Cleopatra had to escape to the nearby country of Syria. While she was there, she raised an army to fight her brother. It could all have ended badly if someone hadn't arrived to take care of the mess."

"And who was that?" asked Digby and Hannah together.

"The great Roman general Gaius Julius Caesar, that's who," said Mr. Rummage triumphantly.

"Julius Caesar!" exclaimed Digby, "so where did he come from?"

"He came from Rome, stupid," said Hannah in disgust.

Mr. Rummage looked first at Digby, then at Hannah. "Not so fast," he said, "Caesar didn't come directly from Rome. He came straight from battle to collect a huge sum of money that Cleopatra's father owed him. Caesar was always short of money."

"Now who does that remind me of?" said Hannah looking at her brother.

"Anyway," continued Mr. Rummage, "when Caesar ordered Cleopatra and her brother to meet with him, she knew she couldn't trust her brother to do the right thing. So that night, she ordered one of her servants to smuggle her into Caesar's heavily guarded palace—wrapped inside a rolled up carpet."

Julius Caesar

Julius Caesar, who fell under Cleopatra's spell, was a tough, no-nonsense soldier in his early fifties who had conquered half the world. He was a brilliant leader and a great athlete. In battle he proved himself to be brave and cool-headed—and his soldiers loved him. But, he was a tricky and ruthless politician who liked a good time—especially with the ladies. He threw his money away on gladiators, banquets, and battle games.

Caesar was tall and elegant with a fair complexion. His deep-set eyes and thin lips gave him a hard, determined look. As he got older he lost hair, which worried him because he was vain. This may have been why he combed it forward in a sort of Roman "comb-over" style. But he needn't have worried—it was almost certainly his power and position that Cleopatra was attracted to!

CONQUEROR OF EGYPT

When Ptolemy saw Cleopatra had won the support of Caesar, he was furious. He fled from the palace on his chariot and raised an army together with his other sister, Arsinoe. But Caesar had a plan. One night he sailed out of the harbor under cover of darkness, pretending to leave the city. But he soon returned with more troops and took Ptolemy and the Egyptian army by surprise. After a two-day battle, the Romans won. Many Egyptians tried to escape by boat, including Ptolemy. But he was drowned—probably dragged underwater by his heavy armor.

CAESAR WAS IMPRESSED BY CLEOPATRA'S COURAGE AND DARING. BUT HE WAS PROBABLY ALSO ATTRACTED BY HER WEALTH AND WHAT SHE COULD DO FOR HIM IN A HOSTILE COUNTRY. AS FOR CLEOPATRA, SHE WAS MORE THAN HAPPY TO HAVE CAESAR AS HER PROTECTOR. THEY WERE MADE FOR EACH OTHER!

Just then, Chrissy from the Genuine Vintage Clothing stall stopped by.

"Telling another of your stories, Mr. Rummage?" she asked, glancing at the children.

"Cleopatra," said Digby. "He's telling us about Cleopatra."

"We're at the part where she fell out of a rolled up carpet, all dusty and crumpled and captured Caesar's heart," said Hannah.

"Looking fantastic, more than likely," laughed Chrissy. "Cleopatra was a real princess, so she'd have known how to look her best to get Caesar's attention!"

"But she didn't have stuff back then to make her face and hair look good, did she?" asked Hannah.

"Of course she did," said Chrissy. "Women in Egypt practically invented makeup."

"That's right," continued Mr. Rummage. "But Cleopatra wasn't just a pretty face. We don't know exactly what she looked like, but she probably had olive skin and dark hair like most Greeks. But she needed a lot more than good looks to influence the great Julius Caesar."

"Apparently," he continued, "she spoke very good Latin, so that was a plus. And she was charming, witty, and made all the right moves. But she also knew how to party. Her banquets and boat bashes were world famous."

"Wish I'd known her," sighed Digby.

Beauty queen

Like many modern women, Cleopatra liked to look her best at all times. To do this she used a variety of cosmetics and wore a heavy wig. Wigs were made of sheep's wool and were often braided at the back and dressed with brilliant jewels.

FRAGRANT BATHS

While ordinary Egyptians washed in the Nile, wealthy Egyptians such as Cleopatra enjoyed the luxury of a bath. After being scrubbed with a mixture of honey, oil, and lime juice, servants wrapped her in linen towels and then massaged fragrant oils into her skin. Afterward, orange henna dye was used to decorate her fingernails.

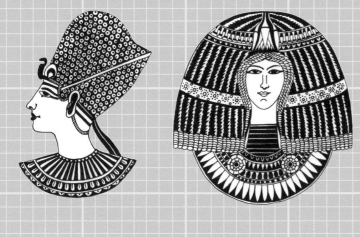

EXPENSIVE MAKEUP

Cleopatra's makeup was made from plants and minerals, such as copper ore and lead ore that were mixed with water. A gray mineral called galena was crushed to make black eye paint, while iron oxide made colors for eyes, lips, and cheeks. Like most Egyptian women of high rank, Cleopatra would have used perfumes made from cedar wood oil or cinnamon, honey, and myrrh. Her makeup was kept in pretty pottery containers.

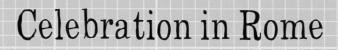

EGYPTIAN TRIUMPH

Back in Rome, Caesar prepared to celebrate his Egyptian conquest by organizing a "triumph," which was a festival where prisoners, loot, and money gained from his battles were paraded through the streets. He summoned Cleopatra to Rome so he could show her off. The Romans were dazzled by the spectacle: there was a golden statue of the Nile god, a model of the Pharos lighthouse, and many exotic animals, including a giraffe.

EXOTIC CELEBRITY

Many Roman people were offended when Caesar put Cleopatra in one of his luxury villas. They thought her manners were strange and they didn't like her self-important ways. She lived extravagantly, throwing parties and giving Roman nobles expensive gifts to win them over to her side. Like celebrities today, she attracted a lot of attention.

DEATH OF CAESAR

Caesar finally met his end in 44 B.C. He'd always had many enemies. Some Roman senators feared that he wanted to be the king with Cleopatra as his queen. They, however, wanted Rome to remain a republic without any royal rulers or dynasty. They **assassinated** him on March 15, a date celebrated as the Ides of March.

"So Caesar had Egypt under his power," said Digby. "But why didn't he just make it a Roman province?"

"He could have," answered Mr. Rummage, "but he so admired Cleopatra, that he wanted to make her queen of her own country instead."

"Why didn't he marry her if he thought so much of her?" asked Hannah.

Mr. Rummage grinned mischievously. "Because he was already married—to Calpurnia. But he was Caesar and could do what he wanted. Besides, he considered himself a descendent of the goddess, Venus, which made him part god too. And with Cleopatra being a descendent of Isis and part god too— they were made for each other."

"Did they really believe all that stuff about being gods?' asked Digby.

"Maybe not, but they certainly knew how to use it in their favor. Anyway, when Caesar returned to Rome he called for Cleopatra, their little son Caesarion, and Cleopatra's young brother to join him.

Cleopatra was given one of Caesar's houses. Then, in the main square, he dedicated a temple with a statue to the goddess Venus and beside it, he erected a golden statue of Cleopatra to show that both he and she were divine beings."

"Wow, it must have been fun playing a divine being," laughed Hannah.

"Hmm, I suppose so, but it didn't last long," continued Mr. Rummage. "Caesar was suddenly assassinated by his own countrymen."

"Oh no! Poor Cleopatra. What did she do?"

Bremen Public Library

"Well, Cleopatra was never short of ideas," said Mr. Rummage. "Especially when she was in danger. Most likely, she turned to the Roman general, Mark Antony, for help because he'd been Caesar's friend. He'd also become the most powerful man in Rome and held Caesar's will."

"Was Cleopatra in it?" asked Hannah.

"No, Octavian, Caesar's nephew, was declared his heir. There was nothing for Cleopatra or Caesarion."

"That was mean, all things considered," said Digby.

"You're right, but Cleopatra had far more important things on her mind—Mark Antony, for one..."

MARK ANTONY WAS AN EXPERIENCED SOLDIER WHO HAD SPENT MOST OF HIS LIFE FIGHTING MILITARY CAMPAIGNS.

TOUGH SOLDIER

Mark Antony was born into a rich Roman family and was friend and first lieutenant to Julius Caesar. It's possible that Cleopatra met Mark Antony when a Roman army restored her father to the throne of Egypt when she was a girl. He was a cavalry officer at the time. But after the three years of civil war in Rome that followed Caesar's death, Mark Antony controlled the whole of the Mediterranean region. He was just the man Cleopatra needed to support her.

Mark Antony

Mark Antony was a tough and ruthless soldier who won many battles for Rome. But he also liked to enjoy himself, and had a weakness for wine, women, and song. When Caesar was murdered, he built up a fortune through crooked deals and forging state documents. It was said that if anything in the empire was for sale, it could be found at Mark Antony's house! He had estates, privileges, titles, taxes, towns, and even provinces. Everyone wanted to be Mark Antony's friend—except one man, and that was his rival and Caesar's heir, Octavian.

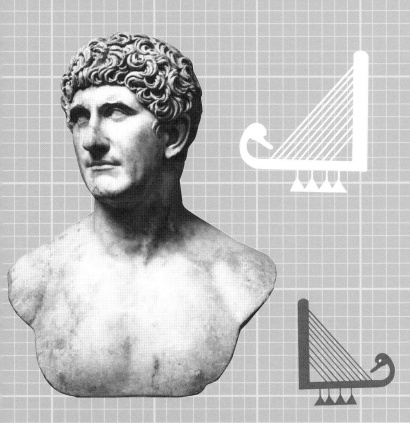

MARK ANTONY WAS PROUD OF HIS FINE FIGURE AND STRONG MUSCLES. HE LIKED TO DRESS LIKE THE LEGENDARY GREEK HERO, HERCULES.

FUN GUY

When Mark Antony entertained Cleopatra, he spared no expense. Even so, his feasts didn't match up to Cleopatra's banquets. In fact, the historian Plutarch said Antony often behaved with "rustic awkwardness" on royal occasions. But Antony didn't mind. He laughed at his own ways, and so did Cleopatra. She knew just how to treat this Roman—although he was very different from Julius Caesar.

THE NEW DIONYSUS

Dionysus was the Greek god of wine and pleasure. Mark Antony, who liked to party, called himself the New Dionysus. This title fitted perfectly with the kind of image he wanted to create as he wined and dined Cleopatra on her royal boat near the city of Tarsus.

Cleopatra sails in

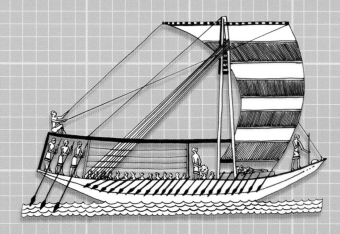

When Cleopatra learned that Mark Antony wanted to meet her, she knew that she had to really impress him. Of course, Cleopatra knew what Mark Antony was like and this influenced her choice of transportation. If the great Roman general wanted to play at being Dionysus and have a good time, that's what she would give him. She planned a dramatic arrival, which Antony would never forget. If her plan worked, she would soon have yet another Roman leader by her side who would marry her and let her keep the Egyptian throne.

THE GOLDEN SHIP

Cleopatra didn't set out for Tarsus with just one boat. She sailed with a fleet that included escorts and supply ships. The royal boat itself was covered in beaten gold so that the sun reflected off it with dazzling light. The purple sails were made of silk and dipped in perfume so the wind wafted the scent of them across the water. Glistening silver oars powered the vessel, while the oarsmen rowed to the sound of flutes and panpipes. This wasn't just a ship, but a floating palace!

THE NEW VENUS

Cleopatra sat on a canopied throne wrapped in veils that swirled like a golden cloud around her. To keep her cool, slave boys dressed like cupids fanned her with exotic plumes and peacock feathers. Her female servants sat around, posing as spirits called Graces and Nerieds, scattering rose petals. They were also ready to offer her sweet treats at the snap of her fingers. Cleopatra was no longer called Isis, but Venus, the goddess of beauty and love—a fitting mate for Mark Antony, the New Dionysus.

FABULOUS FEAST

Inside the royal ship, the walls of the dining area were hung with mirrors and rich tapestries, and hundreds of tiny oil lamps made flickering patterns of light. The air was fragrant with incense. A pair of dining couches were ready for Cleopatra and her guest to lounge on. Next to each couch was a table laid with a golden goblet and dishes of gold set with precious stones. At the end of the banquet, Mark Antony was presented with the plates, goblets, and even the couches as gifts from Cleopatra.

THE PEARL

Cleopatra kept Mark Antony interested with party tricks. Once, she took off one of her huge pearl earrings and plunged it into a goblet of vinegar where it dissolved. Then she drank the contents to show Antony just how wealthy she was—rich enough to destroy a pearl of great price on a whim.

"I guess Mark Antony just couldn't resist," said Digby, looking slightly dejected. "But I would have."

"Who'd put on a banquet like that for you?' said Hannah scornfully.

"Anyway," Mr. Rummage went on, "now that Antony realized just how powerful and wealthy Cleopatra was, he decided he needed her on his side if he was going to defeat Octavian. He rushed to join her in Alexandria."

"I bet she was in charge of him," gloated Hannah.

"Pretty much," said Mr. Rummage. "But after a winter in Egypt, Antony was called back to Rome. He ended up marrying Octavia, Octavian's sister."

"I don't believe it," groaned Hannah, "what did Cleopatra do? It sounds just like a television soap opera."

"A soap opera on the world stage," grinned Mr. Rummage. "Cleopatra could have been devastated. But she was strong willed and decided to wait for her moment."

"I'd have gotten rid of him," said Hannah with a scowl.

"Well, she was right to wait. A few years later they met up again and Cleopatra agreed to help him defeat Octavian so they could rule the world together.

Don't forget, she was determined to save Egypt from Rome.

Their big chance came in 31 B.C. when their fleet of ships finally met up with Octavian's army at Actium. But things started to go wrong for Mark Antony. About two hours into the sea battle, the Egyptian fleet hoisted its sails and headed south. When it was safely away, Antony boarded a smaller boat and went off to join it. But his own fleet stayed behind and was defeated."

"So Antony had planned to run away all along," suggested Hannah.

"Looks like it. By then he knew he couldn't win and was just hoping for the chance to fight another day. A chance that never came."

The Battle of Actium

While the final preparations for war were being made, Mark Antony and Cleopatra decided to have a huge party to celebrate their hoped-for victory. While others worried over battle plans, the happy couple sailed to the island of Samos where they invited all their friends to join them. For days the island thrummed to the music of flutes and harps.

WINDS OF CHANGE

When Marc Antony's fleet faced Octavian's at Actium, the wind suddenly changed direction. But it was too late to retreat. His ships couldn't sail fast enough to charge the enemy which gathered around them like flies. Soon, Octavian's men pressed down on them with spears and flaming missiles. It was only a matter of time before Octavian won the battle.

CLEOPATRA'S LAST STAND

When Cleopatra realized she could no longer rely on Mark Antony for help, she drew up a plan to set up a new kingdom in the East. She even started to build ships and have them dragged across the desert from the Mediterranean to the Red Sea. But Arabian clans from Petra found out about her intentions and burned her docks. It was the final blow to her last bold move.

Illustrirte Weltgeschichte II.   Leipzig: Verlag von Otto Spamer.

Kleopatra während der Schlacht bei Actium.
Zeichnung von Hermann Vogel.

Cleopatra's death

Cleopatra knew that she would soon die. She had already built a magnificent tomb and organized her own funeral feast. When the Roman troops arrived, they surrounded her tomb and kept her prisoner there. Cleopatra told Octavian she was prepared to give up her crown if he let her children govern Egypt for Rome. But he wouldn't agree, so she decided to take her own life. She couldn't bear to see her beloved kingdom ruled by Rome.

CLEOPATRA'S BODY WAS LAID IN A PAINTED COFFIN, READY FOR HER JOURNEY TO THE AFTERLIFE.

CLEOPATRA WAS PROBABLY BURIED IN STYLE, TOGETHER WITH HER TREASURED POSSESSIONS.

COFFIN FOR A QUEEN

Cleopatra's tomb has never been found. But she was probably prepared for burial according to ancient Egyptian customs. First, her body was washed with perfume and covered with herbs and spices to stop decay. Then she was wrapped in linen bandages, with good luck charms placed between the layers. Finally, coins were laid over her eyes and a death mask put over her face.

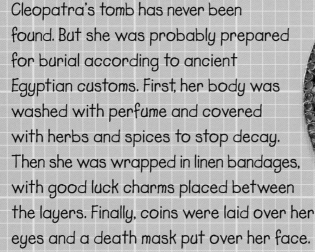

"When Mark Antony arrived back in Egypt he was devastated," said Mr. Rummage sadly. "Everything he and Cleopatra had worked for had vanished."

"Seems like he only had himself to blame," said Hannah.

"Yes, Antony did blame himself. In fact, he threatened to commit suicide when he learned that his troops had gone over to Octavian's side."

"I'll bet Cleopatra wasn't about to give up, though," said Hannah, defiantly.

"No, she was courageous and realistic to the end. She probably realized that Antony couldn't be of use to her any longer. She may even have thought it wise for him to fall on his sword, as a defeated Roman general was expected to do.

Later, he apparently received a message that Cleopatra had killed herself. It wasn't true, but it was the last straw for Mark Antony, and this time he really did fall on his sword. The thrust didn't kill him, though. He was carried on a **litter** to the queen and died in her arms."

"Poor Antony," declared Digby.

"And now it was Cleopatra's turn. She had already prepared herself and decided that the poisonous bite of an asp was the least unpleasant way to die."

"What's an asp?" asked Hannah.

"We think it's an Egyptian snake—a cobra—like the one on her crown.

Octavian wanted her alive, so he could drag her through the streets of Rome in a "triumph". He put guards at her door, but she tricked them and had the snake brought to her room in a basket of figs. Servant women dressed Cleopatra in her finest clothing. They also took poison. Later, Cleopatra was found dead with two small marks on her arm. Octavian buried her with Antony, as she had wished."

"What a story," sighed Digby.

"What a woman!" said his sister.

Digby took the Egyptian coin from Mr. Rummage and thanked him.

"I'll treasure this as one of my greatest antiques," he said, looking at it admiringly, "and remember the great story behind it…"

"Except the part about marrying your brother," said Hannah. "Other than that she was a great queen—and certainly nothing like what I expected."

"Those Roman historians have got a lot of nerve," added Digby. "They really made Cleopatra look bad, didn't they?"

"Yes, but when you look at the facts, as much as we know them, something like the true person comes out," said Mr. Rummage.

"Certainly does,' agreed Hannah.

Then she and Digby turned to go. They waved goodbye to Mr. Rummage and said they'd see him next week.

"You know," said Digby as they walked down the street, "she's not at all like I thought. I imagined her as a selfish, cunning person who wanted everything and cared for no one but herself. I was wrong."

"She was a queen," said Hannah, "a courageous and clever one. She didn't do things just for herself. She did what she could to keep Egypt out of Roman hands and to give her children a future. Its too bad that she failed."

"Still," said Digby, "she led an amazing life, didn't she? I can just imagine that golden ship, and the time when she rolled onto the floor in front of Caesar."

"And her death," added Hannah. "in a way she won that one, didn't she? Octavian didn't get to parade her through Rome as his slave, after all."

"She got the better of him in the end." agreed Digby.

"Good thing too!"

Cleopatra's children

After Cleopatra's funeral, Octavian put Cleopatra's son Caesarion to death. He took Mark Antony and Cleopatra's twin children back with him to Rome, where they were raised by his sister Octavia. Instead of making Egypt a province of Rome, he kept it as his own so that the Caesars who came after him were called the "Kings" of Egypt.

 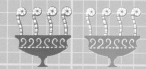

The truth and the legend

Cleopatra was the last pharaoh of Egypt and one of the most fascinating women in history. Her life has been portrayed in poems, plays, and paintings. But many details of her life—including her thoughts, plans, and actions are still a mystery.

Historical accounts of her life have either been lost or cannot be trusted. Most writers of the day were loyal to Rome and so had a poor opinion of her. Only a handful of coins and a few broken statues survive to remind us of how important she was.

 IT IS DIFFICULT TO UNRAVEL THE TRUTH FROM THE LEGEND, BUT HERE ARE SOME OF THE FACTS AND THE FICTION OF CLEOPATRA'S AMAZING STORY:

FICTION: Cleopatra was an Egyptian.
FACT: Cleopatra was a Macedonian Greek. Her family, the Ptolemies, descended from one of Alexander the Great's generals.

FICTION: Cleopatra was a selfish woman who only wanted power and riches for herself.
FACT: Cleopatra was devoted to her country. She did all she could to stop Egypt from falling into the hands of the Romans.

FICTION: Cleopatra was only interested in feasts, fashion, and having fun.
FACT: Cleopatra was a brilliant politician. She used her feminine charm to influence powerful men so she could protect her children and her country. She was probably more interested in making alliances than in affairs of the heart.

FICTION: Cleopatra had an only child, called Caesarion.
FACT: Cleopatra had four children. Ptolemy Caesar, or Caesarion, was Caesar's son. Cleopatra Selene, Alexander Helios, and Ptolemy Philadelphus were all Mark Antony's children.

FICTION: Cleopatra allowed her heart to govern her head.
FACT: Quite the opposite, her head was always in command of what she did.

FICTION: The Romans thought that Roman rule would have civilized Egypt.
FACT: Egypt, and particularly Alexandria, were far more cultured than Rome. The Romans were considered barbarians by the sophisticated Egyptian court.

Glossary

alabaster A kind of white stone

assassinate To murder a famous person by surprise attack for political reasons

bribery Offering money to someone in order to influence him or her

corruption Dishonesty

drought A long period of very low rainfall, especially one that harms crops or living conditions

litter An enclosed or curtained couch mounted on two parallel bars and used to carry royalty

lute A pear-shaped stringed instrument

lyre A stringed instrument of the harp family having two curved arms connected at the upper end by a crossbar

Macedonian A person from Macedonia

merchant A person who buys and resells goods to make money

onyx A valuable dark-colored gem

scepter A staff held by a king or queen as a sign of authority

Index

Other characters in the Stories of Great People series.

KENZO the barber has a wig or hairpiece for every occasion, and is always happy to put his scissors to use!

SAFFRON sells pots and pans, herbs, spices, oils, soaps, and dyes from her spice kitchen stall.

BUZZ is a street vendor with all the gossip. He sells treats from a tray that's strapped around his neck.

COLONEL KARBUNCLE sells military uniforms, medals, flags, swords, helmets, cannon balls—all from the trunk of his old jeep.

YOUSSEF has traveled to many places around the world. He carries a bag full of souvenirs from his exciting journeys.

PIXIE the market's fortuneteller sells incense, lotions and potions, candles, mandalas, and crystals inside her exotic stall.

Mrs. BILGE pushes her dustcart around the market, picking up litter. Trouble is, she's always throwing away the objects on Mr. Rummage's stall.

PRU is a dreamer and Hannah's best friend. She likes to visit the market with Digby and Hannah, especially when makeup and dressing up is involved.

JAKE is Digby's friend. He's got a lively imagination and is always up to mischief.

Mr. POLLOCK's toy stall is filled with string puppets, rocking horses, model planes, wooden animals—and he makes them all himself!